MW00473330

My Moon,
My Light

Juliet Barriffe

ISBN 978-1-63903-751-3 (paperback)
ISBN 978-1-63903-752-0 (digital)

Copyright © 2021 by Juliet Barriffe

All rights reserved. No part of this publication may be reproduced, distributed, or transmitted in any form or by any means, including photocopying, recording, or other electronic or mechanical methods without the prior written permission of the publisher. For permission requests, solicit the publisher via the address below.

Christian Faith Publishing, Inc.
832 Park Avenue
Meadville, PA 16335
www.christianfaithpublishing.com

Printed in the United States of America

Taking It from Here

There is something about the moon, specifically the full moon, on a dark night. Its glow generates way up there in the sky. This passion that I developed for the moon from my childhood days came with my admiration of the one that's greater than us. He placed the sun, the moon, and the stars in the sky. Oh, the sky! Have you ever looked toward the sky on a nice sunny day? There you will see the clouds displaying its artworks. Formation of various things with the likes of a horse, angels, sheep, dogs, or fish can be seen there in the clouds depending on one's eyes and imagination. How about the stars? They appear as countless twinkling candle lights that shine so bright, as it did when it guided the wise men to baby Jesus. Then there is the sun that appears in the mornings and leaves us at dusk. The sun does play a vital role in our way of life; we do depend on it at a balance scale to make things flourish for us. The sun, moon, and stars, along with the sky, all serve their purpose in our world. Some people are fascinated with one or the other. But I gravitate to the moon.

There are times that I become overzealous with passion to the extent of trying to engage my daughters at an early age in my interest and admiration for the moon, but my girls only make mockery of me. "Mommy! It's just the moon, it's nothing more."

They hadn't seen the beauty. They had not found that awe in their heart to the privilege and gratefulness of God's gift of sight to see what I see in it. Today they are older and have come to the acceptance that there is something special about the moon.

The moon for me is just one more reason to give reverence to the Most High God for all His gifts to us. I thank Him for my eyes, for without them I would not be able to gaze upon the moon with such passion and see the beauty of it that allows my heart to be overwhelmed with praise. I became a child in my simple beliefs that the moon follows me wherever I go. I gravitate to it, trusting that with the light of the moon my path is lit and my shadow becomes visible. In my young adult years into my mature adult world, I overly romanticized in my heart the desires of strolling along with my hand clasped in that of the one who shares my sentiment and passion of the moon to make walking meaningful by the light of the moon. There is something about the moon that captivates my emotion. Could it be, I wonder, at times if it is the energy that generates from the sun which makes it gravitating and tingles my emotion to the extent of praising and worshipping God? And there in my joy the desire to sing and dance by the light the moon gives us. In my heart of love and compassion I am not able to associate any negative traits with the moon. For me it is an old folktale, the saying of people behaving strangely and doing crazy things whenever there is a full moon. As for myself I only see it for what it is—beautiful. Its beauty, whether it is half-moon, quarter moon, *U* shape, and its other different shapes, is breathtaking knowing that God placed it in the sky and allows that one object to display its many splendor. And yes, there are times that the moon seems to be absent from the sky, maybe! Just maybe it is then that it is taking its rest so that when it comes forth it would show off one of its unique form. One of which I was blessed to witness for myself in the month of September of the year 2015 when the moon became red (blood moon). To me it was a beautiful sight to behold, and the transformation that took place and only lasted for a few minutes, it's an opportunity I may not get to witness again. Therefore, my heart rejoiced of the experience.

Over the years, many feelings have engulfed me and placed my emotions in a poetic mood, having words flowing and coming together in my mind and in my heart. This pureness of God's gift to me has often left me questioning the hardness of man's heart toward the designer and orchestrator, the one who is able to do so great and unimaginable things. I am not lacking the knowledge that we have been granted free will to believe and trust Him or do the opposite, which is snaring upon Him and refusing to embrace His grace and compassion, which allows us to be content and receptive of the beauty which He has bestowed upon us. It has been said that beauty is in the eye of the beholder. However, that beholder should have peace, which will allow him or her the extent of such beauty.

However, with that beauty we should not be conceited, self-centered, and condescending. There are times that I have conflict of emotions, sadness, regrets, loneliness, and the famous phrase "tired of being tired." And there are times I would face some conflicting emotions mentally, but I try not to be consumed by it due to the love of self.

Yes, my self-love keeps me intact, because I speak to myself. I reason, I console, I encourage myself that whatever it maybe, it is not worth losing me. If I lose my mind I will be losing identifying with whom I am. I appreciate the scripture in Luke 12:25 that brings light to the concept of overly exalting oneself with worry. For me, it means, why worry about things you cannot change? Overall, I would like to give all of the credit to my Creator for always being there to comfort me. Many times I thought that I will not make it, but somehow, out of nowhere, I would get jerk back to reality, and so I would resurface with gratefulness. During such period of time I would reflect on nature's beauty and God's grace, which leads me to admire creatures and plants great and small—such as the sound of the birds which speaks of joy, the butterfly's freedom, the various colors of flowers reflecting radiance, the breeze of breath, the rain of cleansing—and I gather it all up in my heart and thank the Lord for allowing me to be alive that I can honor His gifts so wonderful designed for us and its beauty to behold.

When our Father created the heavens and the earth it was all pleasing to His eyes, and He acknowledged He has done a good job.

He has done such a good job. My physical being regrets that one day I would be leaving it all behind, but then mentally I am looking forward for that day when I will be able to see and say thank you to our King for all He has done and given us. Therefore, when I look upon the moon I am reminded of our Father's love. You may be wondering how is it the moon reminds her of the Savior's love? You see, the moon comes out at night. There are times that it is not visible and darkness prevails over the land, and during the times the moon shines there is a glow on the land. In our lives when darkness takes over, our direction and journey become challenging, but when you find favor you become lighthearted. That's the light. The freedom of seeing and knowing where you are going. The moon reminds me of His love for us, our Savior's love that is unconditional. Without His love and favor, we would be in darkness all of our life. Look, He suffered pain and abuse for us. Oh my! He even died for us that we may live. Yes, live a life filled with abundant blessings and a gift of light. And all we need to do is receive it all with great appreciation; it's free, all free.

These are my thoughts, my views. This is my take and how I perceive the awesomeness of our Savior's gifts to us. Therefore, in the light of the day when the sun shines on the land, I say, "Thank you, Lord." And when darkness overcomes the day and the stars and moon appears, I often take a deep breath and lift my hands and thank my Savior blowing Him a kiss with a big smile on my face. That's how grateful I feel. Call me crazy if you will. As for me I will say I am in love with my Lord.

In the mornings when I open my eyes I give thanks to the great I AM for allowing me to see a new day. It is strange that as frightening as the world becomes, it is a blessing to be awakened each given day to embrace the day and life. Have you ever wondered about the world and us living in it? The life of people in their part of the world, their everyday living, the way they toil, and their means of surviving. With the internet around we do manage to get a glimpse of what man allows us to see, yet I am curious of what I am not seeing.

The world as we know it is a great and wonderful place, we say, and it is rightfully so. And we all are trying to find our place in it, one way or the other. For some it is a golden pot that one can reach in and comes up abundantly blessed for life. They are the ones who seem to see their names written on everything and just reach out and take. And there are those who will climb the mountains of life and do whatever it requires to stay there. They work hard, sacrifice family and friends; they do not see the flowers nor smell the fragrance; they snare at people who takes time out to play. Their only aim is to reach the top and will work twice as hard to stay there. There are others who look to the hill while working and praying help will come. These are the ones who toil sunup to sundown just to make a life for themselves, praying and hoping that God will make a way for them someday. Now there are those who sit in the valley hoping that blessing will fall on them. These are the people who do not dream or put their strength in toiling. They only wait to be rewarded. No matter what category we are in, in this world it requires faith and belief, along with prayer, to achieve and get to that point we would like to reach.

I have placed myself in the category as one who looks to the hills and pray with the acknowledgment that by faith and belief, all my needs will be taken care of by Daddy O, accepting the fact that by the sweat of my brows I will not go hungry, my hands should not be idle while I wait on the Lord. There is nothing wrong in climbing to the top of the mountain, but one has to be mindful that it's by the grace and mercies of the Most High that we are granted such privileges. It is with worthiness and not with an entitlement's mentality that we should adapt to the blessing for betterment. You see, when Christ took the weight of the world upon Himself, we inherited grace. He paid the price of our predicaments into worthiness, which is privilege rather than entitlement.

I will say that I am a dependent person, but what and whom I am depending on makes a difference to my life. I am worthy because my heavenly Father makes it possible for me to be. Therefore, I depend on Him to take me through my journey in life. And when I look around me and see the wonders of His magnificent gifts in the design of nature, I applaud Him for thinking of me, of us, that we needed beauty to distract us when the ashes are on us. It gives me greater appreciation also for the verse that says, "He gave us beauty for ashes" (Isaiah 61:3). And I know that He did not take the ashes and gave us beauty for us to be defeated.

There was a time in my life that I was weighed down by pile of ashes and, to be honest, defeated. I felt old and totally depressed, and it seemed at that time that when my moon seems to be full and shining bright in my life, the clouds would come and take my light away and the ashes would start weighing me down more. But I was determined to shed the ashes and to shine within the clouds. I have a master who loves me, and I was determined to love Him in return by doing my best to walk in His will. But the tighter I am with my beloved, I felt more pressured. I struggled with being worthy versus unworthy. And I had to constantly remind myself that I am a *sinner saved by grace*, I am *fearfully and wonderfully made*, and that *there is no condemnation for those who are in Christ Jesus.* I had spent some years with the different stages of the moon in my life. I would have a full-moon period, when everything seems to be bright and embracing. Then there was the half-moon when it was not that great but still hopeful. And there is the quarter moon that leaves me to wonder, will tomorrow be better? All along the way, the clouds interrupted my light. How I cried and I prayed, I also sang and danced for the glory of the Lord. But what I learned is that nothing comes to an end until the Lord says so. I had to let go of some things which included me, myself, and I. When I managed to let go of some things, I became a person with lighter clouds over me but became a self-righteous one who wanted to be perfect. I wanted those around me to be perfect and everything in order. I was that person who truly believes she was acting in the will of God. But through it all, I grew. I became a better stronger me, who wishes the best for everyone and with the mind-set of being a servant of God.

I have grown strong within my journey. I was weak, I must admit. I would shy away from things that I do not know. I was more secure with someone by me. But I found strength one night when my Savior told me to choose life or death. I chose life, and thereafter I feared no longer. I walk with Jesus, and He walks with me. Therefore, I must give the Savior the honor for allowing me the gift of a new life not perfect, but it's a life of possibilities. And so I thank Him that I grew to the point of expressing myself in poetry. When I asked Him for the ability to write like the psalmist David, He placed in my spirit poems that have been recognized. What I am saying is sometimes our clouds are there for our growth. We may not see it at the time, but hold on; it will come. Just remember, make yourself available and ready for the change. I was ready for a change, and now I testify that my Lord took my ashes and gave me beauty, and so I am this person today.

Love! Love has always been my banner, and God became my anchor, because He is love. I have come to the realization that love can also be a crutch that some people use to hurt you, and the term *being God-fearing* is used to deceive you into trusting them. We all have things about us that can turn others away, even when we mean well. I believe, however, things that are done with love should mean we are giving and doing our best in the name of love, which should be the believer's code of honor in representing the captain of our ship, our Savior. I have been hurt by people whom I have trusted, and I guess I have hurt people that trusted me also. But for my part I learned to forgive because of love. And I hope in return I be forgiven. The lack of forgiveness truly can turn someone into a very ugly person. I know because I tried to be such a person a few times and came to the realization that the lack of forgiveness causes pain—pain physically as well as mentally. As for myself I do not like the feeling of pain. Therefore, I make the choice to forgive and be at peace with myself. And to be at peace is a wonderful feeling. To be comforted and be at rest in your mind, body, and spirit is stress reduction, which leads to constant connection with the great King because we cannot do it on our own. I could not have done it on my own if I was not connected to the righteous one who keeps me wrapped in His spiritual embrace. Without His presence in our lives the conning one will keep on nudging at us into getting busy for him, tempting us into picking up what we have thrown away. And there, my friend, is when we should pray for the increase of fate to see us through.

We really do need the increase of faith, along with strength to go through, and not that of ourselves but that of the Most High God. I have been tested and tried. You have been tested and tried. However, everyone's end result is different because our test is not the same, our faith is not at the same level, and very noticeable our journey is on different path. I know mine is. I have said earlier that I am a caring and loveable person, and I truly want to believe that everyone is loving and caring, unfortunately that is not so. I have experienced being the recipient of client wrath a few times from people who are educated and make self-declarations of being a good person. As a caregiver I have encountered people of different backgrounds and personality, as we all do in our everyday lives. There is one thing I often encounter giving care to golden-aged people, more specifically females. A golden-aged female who did not prepare her mind to accept the fact that aging is and will take its course and that all the outer beauty will not remain with her, with the facts that the body will not function the same. A few of these ladies have confessed that they had not thought about aging. Therefore, they rebelled about their aging appearance. They would talk joyously of all the wonderful things and the way they were back then when they had flawless body; now in their golden age and with less appreciation for life as it is, they curse their wrinkled aging body and blame God for allowing such aging process to happen to them after all the good they have done and being good. They were not open to accept the gift of life at such a high number age or receptive of growing old. I believe being God-centered would make a great impact and a better understanding of God's gift of a lengthy life. However, while aging erases the youthfulness from our body, sickness can take away the physical and mental ability to function. As it was for a client I had the opportunity of taking care of. She was not an older woman but a woman in her late thirties with an unhealthy habit. Mary, not her real name, was a believer until she became sick. When she found out she had a life-threatening sickness she became devastated and rebellious. A sickness that required some restrictions that she was not complying to. I was placed on her case as her caregiver. In my opinion when I first started the case she saw me as this petite woman that she would be able to manipulate into doing her bidding. Therefore, I was welcomed by her with open arms (a phrase). As my time with her matured, Mary began to dislike me for the chief reason I would not give into her unhealthy request. I guessed I reminded her too much of who she was and should be in Christ. I was accused of being holy and righteous by her, too happy and humming with joy.

Then one day she told me this: "I did all the right things as a child of God. I went to church. I served Him. I am educated. I am a good person, and this is what He did to me, and you came in here all righteous and all." She voiced her desire not to have me there anymore. I reported this to my company, but I was told to remain in place until a replacement can be found. The following morning, I went to the client's home, and I was refused entrance. Mary did not open the door. A few weeks later she died. Mary knew the master;

however, she believed that all the good she had done, along with being a good person, and the sickness that had befall her should not have been. I guess she did not know that although we belong to the Most High God, we aren't exempt from sickness or death, but what we do have is the comforting arms of the master to see us through, along with faith, hope, and belief that according to His will He will heal or save us from death in that season. What I am saying is, in the case of Mary I assumed she hated and despised me for whom I represent.

I will confess there are times that I too question this walk, this journey, this doing good and being good, but then I come to realize that one will not appreciate the comfort and joy of goodness until bad crosses our path and then we began to yearn for that inner peace and comfort of goodness. Being good and doing good equal inner peace. No matter what the case may be, take joy in being God-centered. Yes, oh yes!

I have also embraced the memory of a mother in Christ who welcomed me and loved me for who I am. My memories of Mother P will always linger in my memory box. I was assigned to Mother P as a short-term caregiver. When I first met Mother P, I was embraced with appreciation. She was comforted with the knowledge that I was there for her because she was restricted physically. We had formed a bond even though I was a younger person than her. Mother P respected my opinion and counsel. She was a child of God; she loved when I hummed or sing songs of praise and read the Bible to her. I received my first study Bible from her. But Mother P had some regrets, and two of them were better management of her time and her health. Mother P told me her story of how she had worked with a company for a number of years, never took time off for vacation, and barely ever called out sick. When it was time for retirement, she booked a two-week cruise as a retirement gift to herself. The week of her retirement her company honored her for her years of service. Mother P was all happy about her freedom and her well-deserved vacation, a cruise.

However, Mother P did not make it to that cruise. She had a massive stroke the weekend leading into her trip. She was left paralyzed, not able to do much of anything for herself. After spending some time in the hospital and then the rehabilitation center, she was eventually sent home to be cared for. It was then I met her. Mother P thought of me as that spec of light in her life that when she need to be cheered up I was there to remind her of the goodness of God. She often said to me, "Take time for yourself and family." It was her way of saying to me, "Take my experience as an example." Mother P was not mad at God; she just honored him for showing her mercy. Many have fallen on their bed of affliction but still hold strong to whom they believe in and serve, while others do the opposite. Why do people blame our Savior for their thorns? Although they know that He has paid a great price with his life that we would not have to suffer, He has been blamed by many because of their sinful nature. Why do we do things that are not pleasing to our Savior? *Sin*, Why do we pray, pray, and pray for forgiveness? *Grace*. His grace. I am one grateful person that God has an abundance of grace and mercy toward us.

I applaud Mother P and others who hold on to their faith despite their struggle with their health or other matters in their lives.

Family and friends, as a matter of fact, people on a hold makes a difference to our place here on this earth. I have taken care of a few people who do not have the support of family or friends. They are alone for some reasons. I cannot begin to try picturing being alone, without family members or a friend stopping by just to say hello. I personally know what it's to have the support of family and that kind of friend. My mothers, who are my birth mom and my stepmom, were a strong support to me when I needed them for comfort and guidance. My stepmother flew from my birth land to be with me and to take care of my first child when I was losing touch with myself; it was a share duty between her and my birth mother. When it comes to friends, I do not have many, but for those that I befriend and befriend me, we bond as sisters. I am aware that there are friends who are for real—the ones who get up-close and personal, the ones who are themselves in your face and behind your back! Like the ladies I refer to as sisters. Yes, the friends who mean it when they said, "I have your back, call me anytime." While it is good to have such friends in our corner, it is also good to be that kind of friend to someone. And

I try my best to be that kind of friend. And yes, there are people who will claim to be our friends and slowly feed you to the dogs. But then it is said that everyone plays a role in our life for one reason or other. My daughters believed me to be too friendly, because I often reach out to strangers. Me? No, not friendly, just being kind and polite.

I am an introvert with the personality traits of an extrovert. I love people, but I do not like being overwhelmed in the presence of a gathering. I believe myself to be shy and reserved, but people view me as a friendly and caring person. And yes, I cannot deny being that person who cares about people, but being friendly, that is in some kind of ways. There is this part of me that does not like to see people with a frown on their face, and if I saw someone with that look, that is saying to me, "Today is not my day." I would get this nudge in my spirit to reach out to that person by extending a compliment or use some kind of comment to get the person to smile a little. I have been to places about business where I would encounter someone who needed a listening ear, and I would consider myself blessed to be there for that person to confide in.

Why do I care so much about giving a listening ear to a stranger who wishes to unload what is on his or her mind and in their hearts? I am repaying what I received. I remember a time in the past when I felt as if my burden was weighing me down and my gateway to release was opening up to others. For my unloading, I would choose strangers. Strangers in my point a view will not be biased in their personal opinions in regards to my topics of discussion. There is one view that I was often left with, and that is people naturally cares. They are not able to do anything about the matter, but I was often left with words of comfort. What would you say, if I should say to you; release equals freedom, that freedom from manipulation of those inner thoughts that lead to no fruitful accomplishments? To achieve that freedom that leads to peace of mind and embrace that spiritual understanding that no matter what, God will take care of it. However, being in relationship with the Savior does bring comfort to the mind, more so if we embrace His free gift of love that gives us that inner peace which surpasses all understanding. And I can truly say that I have found that peace, that peace that surpassed all that understanding that allowed me not to take the things that conjure within my mind too seriously or the negativity that wished to unleashed its burden within me. The achievement of freedom of the mind allows me to be more receptive of the gifts that are placed before me—the gift of grace, peace, and mercy from our heavenly Father.

There are gifts abundant at our availability. We only have to acknowledge and connect to it. I have connected to my gift of loving God, people, nature, and anything that falls in line. I connect to God first, for it is written in the great book, "Love the Lord your God with all your heart and with all your soul and with all your mind" (Matthew 22:37). That's a wonderful gift to have, the gift of love. And with that acknowledgment, I will drag your memory to the introduction of my passion for the moon, that passion that grew over the years of trying to release myself of my inner burden. The moon becomes that visual light that allows me to embrace that spiritual light within me. And now that I have connected with that light, there is no more entertaining the darkness that tried to consume my life, because each day when I awaken and look to the hill from where my help comes from, I became spirit-filled.

There was a time in my life, no matter how I tried to stay in the light, darkness seemed to be all around me. I dreamed darkness; I had visions of being consumed by darkness. There was one dream I had, and in this dream, I was in my wedding dress driving down this darkened road trying to escape. To escape what, I did not know, but all I wanted to do was to get away. But I kept driving down this dark road that led to nowhere. For you to better understand my story within my dream and dreams, it began almost a year after my then husband came to America and over two years of marriage. He came and settled in and became familiar with his surroundings and make connections with his friends. The family values that I grew up with and had hoped to have in my marriage began to seem less valuable because he and I were not on the same path or heading the same direction. Back to my dream. I kept having the same dream for a while, until one night in my dream I thought I was finally making my escape, ha! That was what I believed, that I have gotten away, I was free. But to my amazement, it was not so. I got caught on the way, and I was back where I started.

Throughout the time of my episodes of dreams, I had called my second mom in my native country and told her of my dreams, and she in return told me that she did not like the dreams I've been having and to be careful. A few nights later I had that dream again of a near escape. This time a new phase began after my dreams, the beginning of a series of accidents. The first accident occurred about three days after I had the dream. I was driving on my way to an interview when another driver ran into the back of my car at the stoplight. I became frightened. It was my first car accident, and I had no knowledge of how to handle it. The person that I called was my brother. Why not my husband? Because I already placed in my mind that the dreams I was having was associated to him. Therefore, my brother became my strength. God has blessed me with a brother like none other. He was the person who would drop everything and come to me no matter what the distance maybe. If I called him, he will answer my call. I give God thanks for giving me a brother such as the one I have. I respect him for being the man he is. He had never gone up against my then husband for whatever he may have suspected. He just honored me as a brother would a sister and left it at that. As he is a good brother, he is also very good father, as well as a good husband to my sister-in-law. And I will also state that he is not a perfect man but an honorable one. However, when it comes to my dreams, my brother was never in it as my rescuer.

Thereafter, the first accident, a series of accident, occurred over a two-year period. Each would occur within a day or two after a night's dream of dark encounter. I was in an accident during the time I was pregnant with my older daughter and also when she was just a few months old.

Throughout my periods of accidents, I made friends with the Bible. I made Psalm 91 and Psalm 23 the words that I rely on each night and day to see me through. Within and throughout my time of dark encounter and accidents I did not develop a fear of driving. It became something I had to conquer and be good at. I was suffering with pain, pinch nerves, weakness in my right leg and right arm, not to mention the back pain. The pain in my back was my fear that I would not be able to live a life free of back pain. But even the pain in my back didn't stop me from being around the steering wheel of a car. However, I somewhat gave up wearing heels at the time, and I also did a good job enduring my pain while praying for deliverance from my agony. One year in the season of lent the church that I attend, Springfield Gardens United Methodist Church, held consecration on Fridays for those members who were seeking to get closer with God; it was for us an upper-room experience. It was there on one of those Friday nights, during our upper-room experience seeking God at a higher heights, that deliverance came. I was touched by the Holy Spirit. I felt my body stretched, and I was standing six feet tall in the spirit. My normal height is five feet. I claimed healing and I received healing that Friday night. After that night of my spiritual encounter, I haven't suffer with back problems. To God be the glory!

Today, more than twenty years later, I am troubling with numbness and tingling sensation in my hands and feet and was told by the specialist it all occurs from spasm in my back. The specialist asked, "Are you having back pain?" My answer was "No back pain." I know not what tomorrow brings. If I should wake up one day with back pain I will try and live with it the best way I can, for my Father, my Lord and Savior, has given me what I had asked for for twenty years and more. To Him all praise is due. And He is my friend.

I found a new best friend. It is so strange that one can meet someone, somewhere, sometime in one's life, and yet we never know how important or valuable that person can be to us. Well, that's me and my very, very, very best friend. I know about him from my grandmother, and I met his acquaintance on few occasion in my youthful years. I know that he was a force to recognize, respect, and fear.

I believe, but how much and what did I believe as a child growing up? I believed that I should not take the Lord's name in vain. I believed that I must be loving and kind to others. I believed I should be respectful to my elders. I believed I should not lie or steal. I believed these things as a child, and I still do as an adult because it was rammed in my head. Also, they are values for us to live by. But when I met my friend, when I really came face-to-face with him and was held and embraced by him, I fell in love. I fell in love with an old acquaintance, and it felt fresh, real, and new. He has taught me a lot, but his greatest lesson to me is, "It only takes love." Love me first. Therefore, I went on this love quest, which birthed a new me—more considerate, compassionate, kinder, and more thoughtful, gentler, and loving. However, within and throughout it all I encountered new challenges. Things began to happen in my life, which had me questioning my faith, my journey. I struggled with doing what is right.

With me having a husband who was just there, the direction and dream I have for our kids became a one-person mission. We were changing residence just about every year. After leaving my mother's dwelling where we had lived for six years or more, I had gotten depressed. I wanted stability. I had dreams. I wanted our kids to have what they needed so they wouldn't stray from the values I instilled in them. I struggled with making things right. I was trying to climb the ladder of righteousness and be a better example to my two girls. Hold it! Please, please! I am not an innocent party on all account. I did my share of bad deeds too. And I had my portion of wrongful behavior and actions to deal with. There are no good sins, and I have my share of it. But through it all I have learned to hold on to my Savior even more. In my heart I believed that whatever I do in my life I wouldn't want my kids to be affected by it, and so I handed them over in the spiritual realms to our Savior. When I gave birth to my daughters, I was a happy mother with high hopes for their future. During the dark period of my life, I awoke one day with the urge to dedicate my first daughter to our Heavenly Father after seeing the movie *Menace to Society* because what the movie reflected was not a vision I had for my kids. This took place when she was a wee tot and before her baby baptism. When my second daughter came I followed up in what I did with my first. For me it was all about the kids. And God was true to His promise that He will keep me and He will provide for me. All through my struggles, he kept me; all through my wants and needs, he provided for me. For many years I have attended the same church but never been more than an attendee who went to get the Word and to be of peace. And I was contented being a receiver who was trying to live right and do right, and I was yet to hear a preacher who would speak to my heart that it requires more than just being in church.

In the year 1992, a well fired-up, anointed pastor walked in that church, Springfield Gardens United Methodist, as our new pastor, and I was never the same. He repeatedly gave me food for thought each Sunday. It became clear to me that it requires love, sacrifice, and gratitude to appreciate all that the Lord has done, and for me to be a servant. I joined the church finally and became active among the church body, and God has rewarded me generously by taking care of my kids. They were loved and were taken care of by the church family. They were showered with generosity, and they were verbally adopted by a few of the sisters who were just crazy about kids. It was not just within the church community that I found favor, but also with people whom I took care of. However, my challenges remained. I found myself being happy outside my home and happier at church. Therefore, whenever I found myself free I would take my kids bike riding or picnic or some form of activities somewhere. I was some kind of happy, and I hold on to the words I often heard from my grandmother: "Half or little of something is better than nothing at all." Therefore, I lived my life on a half-happy scale. I kept home, I did.

I kept house with compassion, much pride and my obedience to the value of "Do unto others as you would like them to do unto you." I began once again to identify with me. I found myself and my self-worth. And then I began my duties as a wife and mother with a different mind-set and two main goals in mind, and that is to be an example to my kids. An example that exemplifies that when God is your strength you can go through your struggles on that strength. The other goal may seem like a simple excuse to some people, but for me it makes sense. As a young lady growing up I had set my heart on having a family life as it was meant to be—a husband and wife with their children living together in their love den, with us parents dreaming and working on building upon our dreams for the future. And so I had kind of accepted life with my husband as what it is and do the dreaming by myself and make my children my chief focus and my motivation. Therefore, I made up my mind to live within my situation until God says otherwise. As time continued there seemed to be a reflection of stability, and my heart rejoiced. But the enemy saw the direction things were going, and so he planted his weapon within my pathway. When he discharged it, the effects caused damage that was a great blow to my mind. There was no getting the pieces together; each time I tried it only fell apart because my mind wouldn't let it go. And therefore, the old me started to overshadow the new me. My mountain was getting too high; I just couldn't see over it, but I still hold on to the outstretched arms of my Savior I was hurting; however, I persevered. I prayed for my strength each day, and I wore a shield every day, not allowing people to see beyond it. I tried to have the best smile with a walk and a voice of confidence, but beneath it all I felt like a failure. I was drowning. I didn't want the life I was living. I did not want half of life. I didn't want uncertainty, deception, or deceit. I wanted what my parents have—stability. There was no joy within the earthly me, but the spiritual part of me has music and dance within. And then I started dreaming again, but this time in my darkness there was music of joy and favor.

One night I had this dream that I could not make sense of. I found myself on a train on my way to get my kids from school, which was only a short ride from home. However, I was on this train ride for a long time. The train kept going through dark tunnels with excessive speed for what seemed like hours. I began to worry about the kids and how late I would be getting them, but this train had not make a stop from the time I boarded it. However, when the train finally came to a stop and everyone I believe disembarked, the strangest thing I noticed was I was the only living person, everyone else were zombies. Fright beset me. I began to panic. I was lost. In my dream as I walked along the street crowded with zombies trying to find someone to help me, there was no one but the frightful-looking corpses. Then I remembered to pray for guidance. That's when I heard the voice saying to me, "Open your eyes and look." My eyes were open, but apparently, I was not seeing. But when I did look, there was a tailor shop right in front of me. As I stepped into the shop the only other living person I saw greeted me saying, "I have been waiting for you, what can I do for you?" I told him I just wanted my fare to go home. As he placed the fare in my hand I was home.

Not many weeks later, I was at home one night, and I fell asleep in the living room on the sofa that my husband used to take his pre-sleeps on before going to bed for the night. However, on this particular night he was not home, so I took position on the sofa, and as I lay there I heard the voice telling me to get up and consecrate the house. I did as I was told. By this time I was more knowledgeable to the things of God, being among strong believers. I got my oil and some water in a bowl. I went around the house praying and touching each area with oil and water, until my spirit felt satisfied. The house felt cleansed after that; however, there was this tense feeling within me that seemed to have me down. I tried to make the best of things even though I was conscious of the ugliness and deception that tarnish the love that I tried to establish among us as a family. And then came the third dream more like a vision.

And then once again I laid on the same sofa. This time in my dream I was in a sick state laying there. My husband came into the house. However, he ignored the sick me laying there, and I saw him walked past and he went and get the kids. He then proceeded to the front door with my girls by his side. I tried reaching out to stop him, but he began laughing at me lying there as he went through the door with the girls. This time I heard the voice saying, "Choose life or death. Choose to live or choose to die." I then heard my voice crying out, "I choose life, Lord. I choose to live, Lord." The Lord told me He has given me opportunity to life many times, but I chose otherwise. I awoke the next morning with victory in my spirit. In my heart, I knew what the dream means and also what I should do. Not long after that dream the house was put up for sale. It has become meaningless. However, I tried holding on to sentiment with that love within, but it had lost its luster.

I took a leap of faith trying to recapture me. To identify with myself, I went home to my country. I had to get away. I wanted to retrieve some of what I had with my stepmother and her Jamaican pampering. And looking back maybe I was being selfish leaving my two girls with my biological mother back in the States, but I had to.

I needed to regain my stability so that I would be able to function for them. I was struggling with myself and the thought that I did not wish to be in the presence of the man that was my husband, their father, anymore. Within three months being in my country of Jamaica, I was revived. I started to feel on top of the world, even though I was missing my daughters, missing my church family and friends, and at the same time making foolish decisions and stupid mistakes and also trying to make a business work. It had never occurred to me that I was moving too fast. I wanted to be busy and independent; therefore, I started a gift shop business so that I would be able to exercise my creativeness in making and designing different items. I was excited and proud of myself. I had all this great idea of a flourishing business and thought to myself how proud my kids would be of me having a business of my own.

But my girls were missing me. My older daughter, who was known as an honor student, began to fall downhill with her school-work, and my younger, who was bubbly and full of life, had lost her glow. Although my mother, who is an awesome grandmother, was doing a wonderful job with them, they had started to protest about me not being there for them. In their eyes, their dad was not living up to their expectation of being there for them as they thought he would. As for me, my assumptions of being back home in my country would be good, not only for myself but also for my second mother; however, that was only my belief. It was then that reality faced me. My parents who I thought was getting older and tired did not need me. They were more independent and determined to prove that they were capable to carry on. It seemed that I was the one who needed them more.

And then I became more homesick for America. I then began to turn my focus on pleasing my children and not my ego. I wanted to continue with the business. And therefore, I executed a plan of being an absentee business person, and with the help of a trustworthy family member and a friend, I trusted things would work out the way I had it planned. It was almost three months later after I put my plan into action, I returned to America refreshed and feeling like a new person. I took residence with my mother and my girls. I have recaptured my parental position, and my girls were happy to have me back. Life was not the same as we were on our own, but then it was not strange. It was always us together, the girls and I, and I never had to worry that I would ever lose my girls to their father. No, because he loves to have it as a one man's show. He plays a role in their lives but not a great role. But one thing my kids know is that he is Daddy and he loves them in his own way. For myself, there is a half that has never been told. The business failed. All that I invested in it I had not seen a return on it, but I have learned a life lesson, although an expensive one. If I could reverse time I definitely know what I would change. But as it is, I looked back at my journey in life and think sometimes that if I had not been on this journey, would I be holding onto the greatness of God the way I do? Would I be able to reach this peak of joy and inner peace? And even though I know that I am not right in all my ways, I do hold on to the belief that God is holding me in the palm of His hands.

Today I am loving me even more. I am singing and dancing to the joy and hope for better days. I am tense-free. I stopped dreading the anticipation of a divorce or that my children wouldn't have their father with them. I consoled myself with the fact that he was there in the home with us somewhat for fifteen years for the older child and for the younger twelve years; they have a history to relate to—a history that's not all good and not all bad, but a history of their mother and father with them as a family.

I have started that love-myself anthem. I would remind myself that I love me on a daily basis. I have to love me to love my kids the way I do, and that self-love overflows in loving others. I also developed this pattern that I would go to bed hugging myself good night and whispering sweet thoughts to my heavenly Friend and Father. When I awoke in the mornings I would greet Him with the same passion of love and appreciation as when I went to sleep. This went on a good time in my life, because I felt different everything became more meaningful to me. And therefore, I came to the realization that not because I love my Lord and Savior the way I do, it does not exempt me from additional struggles, sickness, or death. Therefore,

I ask the Lord each day to prepare my heart for whatever may come my way.

Before I was doing things to entertain my girls and to take my mind off my situation. Today God has my back as He has over the years, and I honor Him, He is my life day in and day out. Yes, I still get up-close and personal with Him but not as when I was going through trying to be free from my bandage. After greeting and embracing the presence of my Father, my keeper, my sustainer. I would step before the mirror, greet myself, and thank God for His goodness in my life. I could be dead or mentally challenged, but through it all, God gave me me. Now when I look in the mirror I see beauty; other people may say otherwise, but what I see is God's design that weathers the storm. I do have some flaws, but He loves me just the same. And when I speak to me in the mirror. I would say such things as "Girl, you are looking good for your age, not young as the previous years, but you are still here, and I love you." And with that self-love I continue to live, laugh, and pray.

I am now taking it from here because I realized that I can write my own script or even paint my own picture of how I wanted my life to be, but I have learned that if it was not in God's plan it would not be what I wanted it to be. And I pray my life journey is according to His will.

Today my children are grown and making a life for their selves. I pray that my stories will not be their stories. I want to believe that they are stronger taking on their journey in life than it was when I began my own.

I was not wise to the world and the deception that can befall one when I was growing up. I was strong because of the family foundation I had. However, I became weak when I stood alone and had to face my Goliath. On the other hand my kids are all geared up with experience learned from tools that are available to them throughout their years of growing up, and my lesson of life experience that I gathered over the years, I used as stories to give them insights.

Today, I am stronger, experienced woman looking at life with a different viewpoint and praying for a moon watching partner who stands on a solid foundation with our Lord and Savior. I can say it does feel strange trying to get to know and building a friendship with a stranger, but then we are strangers until the foundation is set. I am healed from my past experience, now I am being cautious. I cannot see the heart of another, but I pray this time I will get it right. That's why I am taking it from here. This time in my life.

And so when I close my eyes, I then open them to the realization that there are much to see, because I am alive. When my nostrils tingle to the smell of this earth that I breath of. I am alive because the fragrance of God is sweet. When my ears hear the silent wind blows. I am alive to the sound of God. When I reach out to touch and embrace with love, I am alive because God is love. When my tongue tasted the sweetness and saltiness of that which is provided for us to feast upon, I am alive because God is a sustainer.

He found me when I was lost, weak, and somehow broken. He blew on me and made me fresh again. Therefore, when I look around me I see God even in the smallest of things. And I love Him.

I remember one evening not so long ago in the month of August. I sat on a balcony of a home on a hill in my native country on a cool summer evening. I focused my eyes on the sky. My mind began to absorb the transition from light to darkness in the sky and amongst the clouds, and the beauty and art works that took place within the changes. The many shades of colors generated in its many forms. The formation that displayed beauty allowed my mind to think in comparison to our life and our journey and transitions through life. Our birth and growth reflect the light and achievements that allow us to shine. As also the darkness that represents our downfalls, which tried to keep us from surfacing. The joy and sorrow of our life all add up to our journey through life. And I love it, nature and all. And so the process of the sky and clouds continue, as will the earth continue its many changes, even after we wither and die like the grass. When we are no more, still God lives on, for He is in everything and everything represents Him, our Lord and Savior.

My Reflections

When the Storm Blew

As I walked through my storm, I held my head up high above my circumstances. You see, it is not my strength that I go through, but that of my heavenly Father. For God's will will be done in my life always.

I must give my Savior the highest praise all the time for embracing me into His holy temple. I have been grafted into the body of Christ, in a fatherly kind of way, by our Father, my Lord and Savior, some years ago. Some years ago, my Savior wrapped His arms around me and gave me the touch of a comfort that He knew that I would one day crave. With that touch, I became a regular church member; however, I did not give my God my all. But as the Bible stated, God is a jealous God. My Savior wanted me to have a relationship with Him, and I knew it. However, me, myself, and I would not let go of self or the things of the flesh.

Therefore, with great dependence on self, my burden got overbearing. With my unbearable burden, I went to Jesus and begged Him to walk with me. I wish that I could say that everything was find and well thereafter. No, it wasn't! As a matter of fact, it was then that my burden felt three times the weight I had. I was worried, but my Savior told me that He will take care of me. Yes, I had a lot of questions as well as flashbacks that allowed me to evaluate my position as a follower of Christ. I realized that I still have things in my life that I have to deal with every day. I will always have one more battle to fight, but then the Lord said that the battle is His. I am just here to witness His miracle on the battlefield of my life.

I am not where I was those years ago. The Lord has moved me to a higher place, not perfect but aiming to do His will. I have gained that peace and joy that surpassed all understanding. My Savior has given me a testimony, and I thank Him for it. It is my story, and it makes me who I am in Christ. No one knows of the half that has never been told. You will understand that it is between my Jesus and me, just as you, my sisters and brothers, do not know the extent of my joy, my sorrow, and my pain. But what you should know is that God is a good God, and He is love.

I Still Have Love

For all the things I have been through, I will always give credit to you, my King.

The good things always seem victorious in my eyes, then I would say God has been at my side.

He has been good and true to His words by rewarding me abundantly.

I will declare joyful freedom of my heart, love and contentment of my life. My Lord has been good to me within my walk with thee.

I am flying high, for my Lord lives within me. There the devil sees me pleased within my Redeemer and King. He stepped into my life to claim the glory that belongs to my Lord by touching areas that has grown strong with my Savior's love.

The deceiver smudged my life with his pleasurable way that he cannot hide. His stroke brought tears of regrets and pain. A burden so heavy that it seems that resuscitation would be in vain.

But the heart rebel and seek to repel that which was not in the making of the heavenly King. Forces of darkness have tried to encamp my joy. However, the greater love entrusted deep within my soul has concurred it all.

For all the things I have been through, I will give credit to thee, my King.

You are the strength in good times and remain the strength in my bad times too. Why had I doubt the resurface of my joy? How could I! when I knew that you, oh Lord, would not let my heart be torn apart with whatever weapon that come against me. The breastplate of your righteous ways shall always be my protection; the whole armor of your righteousness will always be my salvation from the unseen forces, my Lord and King. My life I have given unto thee, my Savior. I have come too far not to stand on your promises of your everlasting love.

Amen.

Life Is a Journey

Life is journey that tosses us to and fro.
Sometimes it's like a dried-out river in time of drought.
Sometimes it's like the ocean rich and strong.
Life is a journey; no matter where it takes you, you will have to survive.
It could be in a jungle. It could be in a pit.
When Jesus is with you it seems like paradise within.
Life is a journey; the passage is free.
Just keep holding to Jesus, and He will see you through.
Life is a journey, so stay on the right route.

Dry Those Tears

Many nights she stood looking through the windows of disappointment, hoping and praying that her now regret would appear as it was before deception changed the rule of a once solid relationship.

Thoughts of many issues captured her mind and tangled her heart.

Tears of regrets became her refuge by day and by night.

An addict whom she became with the warm tears drifting down her face; without it she was uncomfortable, and with it she was pathetic.

A still soft voice shook her tearful world one day with a question she thought not to ask herself: "Why are you crying?"

The question shook the tears from her eyes and filled her heart with love for a situation that was taken care of a long time ago by her Father up above.

The Creation I Adore

I selfishly adore the beauty of God's creation. The unanswered question of the formation of the sky. The flow of the water that drench one part of his world, while the other portion dries out because of the lack of the flowing tears from above.

I selfishly adore the beauty of God's creation. The mountains that rises up as if to touch the flooring of his kingdom.

The stars that shine so bright like the eyes of babies.

The sun that penetrates the earth with its ray in the day, while the moon sits back gracefully awaiting its time to display one of its many shapes.

I selfishly adore the beauty of God's creation.

The Perplexed Mind

The anxiety of the future and the regret of the past has perplexed my mind; though I need not worry of what to come, because the Father has paved the way for me.

The thought of unworthiness became a mind play. The things I should not do and have done have become a burden. The reflection of what is and could be if the Father should step aside and allow it to be, but then the God I serve assured me that nothing that comes against me will flourish.

How weak is the heart, how feeble is the mind, when we give the devil the time of day.

Tell Me, Lord

The changes I asked you for, Lord, are being fulfilled.

The act of kindness, the little touch of love, the smile of confidence, and the spoken words of fun.

Yet I question the genuineness of it all, though I am seeing the Father's work at hand. But my doubt is not of you, Lord, but of man. My trust becomes conflicted, because I have seen man in all his deeds, and he is yet to accept the righteous way of you, my King.

How long will the changes last, I want to know. Is this the will of God or a man acting in a scene he comes to know so well?

The Cry

My God, my God
Do not forsake me
Let not my ignorance and the lack of knowledge
to your words make me not acknowledge you;
Or let me seek refuge in the wrong.
Let me look to the right and see your face
Let me look to the left and see only your face
Let me look to the sky and see you smiling at me
My God, my God
Do not forsake me!
You are my shield
You are my protector
In you I find strength
In you I find refuge
My God, my God
Do not forsake me.

God Knows Best

The words I will to say wont express the way that I feel—the guilt, the blame, and the conviction.

But God knows best.

The things I should have done, the things I should not have done, guess what? The result may have been the same.

For God knows best.

Take your problem to Him and leave it there, because He does not judge but forgives.

Because He knows best.

All burdens you bare, all sorrows and fears, don't you know that Jesus does care! For Him there is no fear.

Just take it to Him, for He knows best.

Jesus does know best.

I Want to Wake Up

I want to wake up to the sun shining through my windows with the promise of prosperity and possibilities.

I want to wake up to the whispering sounds of the birds telling me how good it is to be alive with my senses.

I want to wake up knowing that I am truly loved by brothers and sisters as the Lord said we should.

I want to wake up because the Lord has seen it fit that I should enjoy the beauty of His creations and be blessed by His peace and love upon me.

I want to wake up knowing that I can make a difference by sharing His love and peace that I have found in my Savior.

I want to wake up because God has something for me to do.

I want to wake up, for it's good to be alive with the grace of God.

I Went Home

Where do I go when my back is against the wall and it seems there is nowhere else to walk? My mind sees four walls, and I am in the middle of it all.

Where do I go from here? It seems my only escape is you, oh Lord. I have known you all my life, but I stopped myself from being your friend. Now that I am in the pit of hell, I know that my escape is you, my Lord and friend.

Where do I go from here being set free from my adversity?

Where do I go but home to the church where I first met thee, my rock and my deliverer?

Yes! I am home, Lord, you have set me free. That's where I went from my downfall, home to thee. Amen.

How Do You?

How do you break loose from a bond that is not there?
How do you break loose from a thought that is not clear?
How do you break from a friendship that is so loose? How do you kick your darkest fear?
How do you understand the incomprehensible? How do you love when your heart feels hate?
How do you touch when things seem untouchable? How do you hold on to something that is not there? How do you know you can do all things that seem impossible?
How do you know?
I know because I am a child of the King who makes all things within my life possible.

The Day I Will to See

I woke up today not knowing what will be in my way
I prayed for guidance and protection
Yet I am doubtful about the day
They say it's God's will if I see the ending of the day
But anxiously I also await the following day
But why do I when I am still into today?
There are bills to be paid
There is the house to be cleaned
There are the kids to fuss about
Not to mention the husband who is not around
But, Lord, I prayed, please see me through this day;
Tomorrow will be the same
The bill to pay
The house to clean
The kids to fuss about, and maybe the husband will be around
But, God, it's good when I open my eyes and see the light of day.

The Prayer

Strengthen my mind, dear Lord,
put me back in drive, and I shall
drive myself to do what is right.
The realization of my guilt and
my disobedience of not doing your will
has confused my mind and weaken
my body. Dear Lord, I pray, please
strengthen my mind and put me back
in drive that I may drive myself to do
your will.

I Am Me

I am me because I am me.
I am me because who else
am I supposed to be?
Don't take me away from me.
For I am who I am created to be.
I am me.

The Possibility

Bright lights and candle lights
For me with you will never be, but
I do find comfort in starlight and
moonlight, for it is nature's way you see.
Boardwalk and park walks with you
will never be, but I found joy in
jumping and running, singing and dancing
to my Savior all the way; you see, that's the
way it should be.

The Deception

This heart of mine dance with joy the day
he asked me to be his wife.
Love was not from first sight, but he captivated me
with his charm.
He stood out in my eyes above
other men I knew because he did the honorable
thing.

Like a prince dressed in his armor he went
before my dad, the king.
He passed the test by
doing his best, the right way.
I had admired him then; I would admire him now if he had
kept his armor on.
He did not know he
would be my king.

Where did all his charms go?
Was there no more honor in his being?
A true prince of honor keeps holding onto his claim even
after the great scene.

The Letter

My friends of the past,

I am sorry I don't see you anymore. It's not that I don't care for you all, but I have found a new friend, named Jesus. He hangs out with a different group of friends that I love more. I don't mean to put you all out of my life, but you'll do remind me of my past and the outrageous things I did and said.

My new friend, Jesus, He knows about me and my past, even before I told Him. He told me to let the past remain in the past and let the present be like a guiding star. He is an awesome fellow, my friend Jesus. I would like you to meet Him too.

Maybe one day He will stop by you. He is a busy fellow, my friend, with all the children He has. However, He still finds time for His friends. Oh, there is something else about my friend. He is a humble and loving person. He can captivate the essence of your being without you knowing that He is softening your heart.

My new friend, He asked not for much in return but to love one another as He loves us. I have found life highly rewarding in almost everything I do and asked in the name of my new friend. Let me tell you this the most beautiful thing about my friend. He loves me unconditionally, and He is always ready to forgive if I only go to Him and honestly ask for forgiveness. I remember there were times I messed up with you, and you would not let me forget about it for months. Do you see now why I chose His friendship over yours? He is forgiving, loving, caring, and honest. I just hope one day you will meet Him.

From your ex-friend with love

P.S. I get to understand that my friend stopped by you the other day, but you ignored Him. The next time He stops by, please embrace Him.

Oh, Mighty King!

Oh, mighty King! Oh, Jehovah!
You can't lose your crown for not playing our games; that brought us sin and shame.
You, oh King of eternity, is who we want to be.
But sin and shame, more so guilt, have kept us from hearing thee crying out, "Come to me!"
Oh, mighty King! Oh, Jehovah!
Now tired and heartbroken without a friend to give a helping hand, sad and confused I kneeled to cry away my sorrow and pain. There I heard you say, "Come to me instead."
Oh, mighty King! Oh, Jehovah!
I heard thee crying out to me, "Come, I will be your friend."
Oh, mighty King! Oh, Jehovah!
I thank thee for rescuing me.

The God Who Saves Me

He allowed not my enemies to triumph over me.
He allowed not my fear to encamp me,
When gulf of darkness tried to over shadow me.
My Lord and Savior delivered me from the pit of my enemies.
When the forces of evil tried to take me off the face
of this earth, my Savior turned things around.
I was scratched but not torn.
I was weak, but now I am strong in the knowledge of the Lord.
My darkness is overshadowed by the light of prosperity; the great I Am.
The God who saves me has enlighten my heart with His love.

I Remember

I remember sometimes ago when I was everything
and everybody else was nothing in my eyes
in the world of the have and the have-not.
I considered myself the cream of the crop
with the security of a family and the protection of
my earthly father.
My role I had to play was be the child who loved
and feared the power of her authority.
The privilege was great, and trust was a matter of
worthiness.
Now those days are gone;
I have put childish ways and thoughts away.
I remember sometimes ago when I became
everything and everybody else became everything
in my eyes, in the world of the have and the have-not.
I have learned to serve in the building up of the
kingdom of God.
I have learned to exercise my purpose in loving the
lost sheep and being a light to them.
I remember sometimes ago when I became God's
servant and pledge to do His will in good times and
in bad, in my weakness and in my strength, when
my mountain gets high and my valley gets low;
until the last blow of my breath.
I know that I am nothing if I am not living in His will.
I have surrendered as God's servant.
I remember. I remember I am a servant of the
heavenly King.

Thank You, Lord

I thank you, Lord, for this life that is precious and free.
I thank you, Lord, for allowing me to live life abundantly.
I thank you, Lord! Oh, I thank you, Lord!
I thank you for this life you have given me.
When you gave your life on Calvary you set me
free from a life of sin and condemnation.
I thank you, Lord! Oh, I thank you, Lord!
I thank you for loving me.

My Dreaded Fear

For God hath not given us the spirit of fear; but of
power, and of love, and of a sound mine.
—2 Timothy 1:7

I have a walk of confidence and a challenging persona that gives the idea that I have things under control. But would you believe it if I told you that I am fearful of getting lost? Would you? I guess you would not. However, as a driver I have come to this realization some time ago, that getting lost is one of my biggest fear. I love to drive; I do love to drive. I love to drive to places near and far. It's one of my favorite things to do, away from getting creative in the world of crafts. Within myself it feels good being around the steering wheel of anything drivable on the streets. And also one of my heart's desire is to legally drive at an unrestricted speed. But I guess that would remain only a dream. However, with this passion for driving, I have one setback. I am unable to read the signs while driving, and my chances of missing my exit becomes great, and so the fear of getting lost physically is greater. It also brought on a mental impairment to my thoughts of finding my way out, and that would have me thinking I could end up in a place of no return. This is what my fear does to me. But there is an extension to my fear. I dread the thought of getting lost spiritually also.

First, let me relate this to you. Over the years I have been evaluating myself. I pause for a moment and say this, each of us should take some time in evaluating oneself. And you should try to know you, if not in all things, but in most things. Believe me, you know more about you than the other persons believed they know about you. Anyway, that is what I did, and what I get to realized is that I am most confident in driving when I am familiar with the streets and highways. And if I do not know the route, someone with navigating experience will do me justice. I have tried to overcome this fearful impairment by challenging myself to my first long-distance driving trip as a driver.

It was a beautiful spring morning in June, some years ago. I was with my two daughters and my female cousin, Anne, who tried her best to be my navigator for that trip on our way to Mississauga in Ontario, Canada. It was five thirty in the morning when we started off on our eight hours of drive. It was about five hours in the trip that we crossed over the Canadian border. There and then I thought, *This is good, we will reach our destination on time.* Oh, but six hours later we were driving through areas that were no way close to our destination. For me we were going through no man's land; we were experiencing that wilderness experience. We were driving through miles and miles of road without any sight of life. When we came to a town, we filled the car tank with gas. We had no urge to eat; we just wanted to be on track again. We asked for directions then; however, we were still on the guessing path because the directions that were given seem to put us more into the wilderness. To be honest, the view was not that bad; there were miles of farmlands of different kinds of produce and pastures with cows and horses to be admired from a distant. But then it was not enchanting; we were lost. I became very anxious, and prayer became my source of courage and guidance. After few hours of driving we finally came upon a busy highway with road for the killing. And there we rejoice for the busyness of it, and we were praying and hoping we were on the right path to Mississauga. It was no fun being lost, but the good part of it was I was not alone, and that helped calmed my fear. I had tried very hard to be brave, but deep within my soul I was praying very hard, and I knew that my cousin was doing her part in the prayer department, because when it comes to praying my cousin is one of the person to have on your team. My girls were in their early teens then, and I must say they took it very well because throughout the drive they were asleep most of the time. Well, we did found out that we were on the right path when we stopped for gas and approached some very friendly people for direction. We were hundreds of miles from Mississauga in Ontario, Canada, but it was less stressful. We now have a better understanding of our direction and the availability of our cell phone. A trip that should have taken us eight hours to get to our destination ended up taking us thirteen hours. One wrong exit took us on a drive away from where we should have been within the calculated time.

Did this trip help me to overcome my fear of getting lost? Not really! But what I learned to do was to challenge my physical fear, which also allowed me to look into my fear of getting spiritually lost.

I would hate to wake up one day and realize that the spiritual connection that I have with my heavenly Father is no longer there. Even though I know that He will never leave me nor forsake me. But then it would not be my Father and Savior who will turn His back. I know that for certain. But why then would I be fearful? I am fearful because His love is so great, and I would not like to lose it because of my foolish ways.

There are times foolish actions and thoughts do take place, and there are times that words are not appropriately applied or things seen are not always right. Therefore, I question myself of my faith and my walk. I have often prayed for my Father's forgiveness, and I know that He has granted it due to my breath of inner peace. However, I somehow have that fear that one day He would declare, "Enough is enough. I will leave you to your ways." Then I would know that I would truly be lost without Him. That's why I fear losing my way spiritually. How do my physical and spiritual ways conflict my mind? With my physical fear, it is a matter of the choice I made in driving. I could clearly have someone drive me, or I could use public transport. But because of my passion for driving, I embrace that fear. Whereas, my spiritual fear relates to the love and connection along with my relationship with my Savior whom I would not like to be disconnected from. I have now learned not to be blindsided by my fears by using the tools that are available.

I have learned to use the computer to my advantage. There are websites available with direction. And there is GPS, a special friend to me before I discovered the phone and its features. And direction is accessible by typing in the starting point and point of destination. Thank God for technology. Where my spiritual fear is concerned, there is a tool for that also; and that tool is the Bible. I have known this all my life, that is since I have been thought as a child that "The map of life is the Bible." The Bible is there for me to stay connected by reading the Word and having faith. So why do I fear being lost when I have the map and the author of it in my life? One word: fear!

However, I have come to realize that fear will keep me bound if I am not strong enough to challenge it. Therefore, I need to keep holding on to the Rock that is higher than me. And although our God did not give us a spirit of fear; however, many of us do invite fear into our lives.

My Story

The year was 1984. I was then a young lady full of life and passionately in love with it—love for people and nature. It was the year that I thought that everything good will come my way, because just maybe sometime within the year I would be with my mom in America. Things had begun to change in our household. I was finally getting a bit of freedom to venture out on my own, and so I gravitated to the idea of exercising my young adult privilege by accepting a dinner invitation from my friend and her husband on a Sunday.

It was a bright and sunny Sunday afternoon in January in the city of Kingston, Jamaica. Just as many Sundays before my household activities were the same, with one difference to what we were accustomed to. On this particular Sunday, I will not be a part of the regular routine. While I was getting myself ready for my evening out, my stepmother was in the kitchen, along with my sister and the helper, getting dinner done. The radio was playing some of the well-known songs in that era, and the music never sounded so embracing in a long while to me. I felt no guilt. I am doing something different; I was doing it my way. As I completed my dressing, I took a look in the mirror and liked what was reflecting back at me. The white halter-top blouse rest on my slim body frame along with a white, fitted jeans, a strapped black slippers that stand at two-and-a-half-inch high. I accessorized my dressing with two gold chains of which one was of some value because it has on it a pendant that was costly. Also, a gold watch on my left hand and three gold bracelets on my right. I was pleasing to my eyes. I exited my room to be greeted by the pleasing looks of those who I was deserting, and I know then that I was presentable in a ladylike manner.

My father was launching out on the patio reading the Sunday's newspaper. When I made my presence known to him, he looked up at me and his words were "Watch yourself and those jewelry you are wearing. Enjoy yourself." I nodded my head and sighed a breath of relief that his words were not harsh toward me, and so I stepped out of the presence of what I was accustomed to, with joy bubbling over within me, and I knew it reflected on my face. As I walked along the road to the bus stop, I knew I was admired. Some made it obvious shouting compliments my way, and I smiled. But one admirer that day I will never forget. He did not say a word, we never spoke, but our eyes met and locked. A smile and a nod of approval were all we shared.

I reached my friends home in good time, and we had a wonderful Sunday afternoon, the day I became free. But unknowing to me a day that started off that well will not be ending the same. I departed from my friend's home at a decent time to get the bus home. There was a bit of daylight still in the sky, but darkness was fast approaching. At the bus stop I waited, but no bus came for the longest while. When a bus came it was not the one that would drop me off close to where I lived. It was getting late and I was getting anxious, so I decided on taking the available bus that would let me off about a mile from home. As I stepped on the bus something in my spirit kept telling me not to. However, I went against my feelings. I just wanted to get home at a decent time so that I would be at peace with my father. As the bus approached the stop where I should get off, I clearly heard the voice in my ears say, "Do not get off the bus." What am I going to do? At that point I had no choice but to get off, and so I did.

As I walked the way home in the night the streets were slightly lit with streetlights. As I continued to walk I had this uncomfortable feeling that I was being followed. As soon as I became aware of my followers, it was at that same instance the three men confronted me. They had a gun pointed at me, and they wasted no time to demand my watch. There and then I decided that they will not have it. And so I went into action with the hope that I could manipulate the situation by informing my assailant that the jewelry that I was wearing were not gold. My confrontation with them drew attention from passersby, and one such passersby was the young man whom I had eye contact with earlier in the day. When I saw him standing on the other side of the highway, I did not know what came over me, but as I stood there trying my best not to let the three hoodlums take what belongs to me, I got super courageous just as one of the three grabbed for my chains. I pulled back and it burst in his hand, so I thought. When they told me to take the watch off, I did so, but instead of giving it to them I used that courage I gain and went into action. I yelled to my newfound friend across the highway, "Catch!" I threw the watch to him, and at the same moment I heard his voice yelling, "Run, come!" And I did. I raced across the busy highway without a second thought. As I reached my angel he grabbed me, and we ran into hiding, because my assailant came after us. I looked at my angel, and I saw him searching himself and a look of disbelief on his face. I began to say to myself, "What have I gotten myself into? Have I jumped out of the frying pan into the fire?" As we hid they searched for us for what seems to be hours, but in reality, it was five minutes or less. They eventually gave up and went away.

We came out from hiding from among the bushes by the golly. As we stand in the open, my angel handed my watch to me. He inquired, "Are you okay? Can you get home from here by yourself?" I told him no, and he stopped a passing taxi. Even though I was suspicious of who he may be, I went in the taxi with him. When he asked for my address, I gave it. However, in the taxi on our way to my home, I began to relax with this stranger who became my angel. He told me he was returning home after visiting his friends when he saw me standing with those hoodlums. He became concerned, because when he saw me earlier in the day I did not strike him as the kind of woman who would keep company with those guys. He also told me he was a cop, and for some reason he left his gun. I breathe a breath of relief and thanked God that he was not one of Jamaica's don. As the taxi stopped at my gate, I invited him in, but he declined. I bid him good night and thanked him. I ran inside to the comfort of my home where I related my mishap to my family members without the drama and my close calling to death. At the end of my story I realized that I did not know the name of the man who came to my rescue, my angel.

Oh, my dad he just listened, and at the end he said, "I told you to be careful. Thank God you are okay." When I went to my room to get ready for bed, as I removed my top, out fell my favorite chain and pendant. A scream of joy filled the air; I came out a winner. And I thank God for sending me an angel.

About the Author

A mother of two adult daughters and grandmother of two, I regard her as very unique person, and in my eyes, she is probably one of the most self-less person I know. Once when I was younger I asked her how did she know she would be such an amazing mother, and her response to me was "I made up my mind before I had kids that I was going to be a good mother."

Born and raised in Jamaica, she has strong family values and teachings which she, in turn, instilled into myself and my sister. Our mother is known for her strength. No matter how hard times would get, she would always find a way out. I am proud to have her as our mom. No matter how many sacrifices she has to make, she always made sure that we had everything we needed, and she has lived up to her decision of being a great mom by her dedication to her kids. Another thing about my mom is she strongly believes that the Lord is the director of her life, and it shows in everything that she does. My mom is very talented in my eyes, and she is one of those people that does things with style and grace so effortlessly. Mom will literally give her last to anyone; that's one of the things I admire about her the most. She loves nature just as much she loves people, even though she is somewhat shy and takes some time to warm up to others. Her Christian values had made her outlook on life as "One day at a time." I have always valued her advice especially now at this point in my life. There is one advice she uses from the Bible that stays with me. Mom told us, "Make use of your strength in your youthful days, that when you grow old you will not regret the days which had passed you by." I am the proud daughter of the author of this book.

CPSIA information can be obtained
at www.ICGtesting.com
Printed in the USA
BVHW031401221121
622225BV00003B/147

9 781639 037513